Newport Community Learning &
Libraries

X010597

Community Learning & Libraries
Cymuned Ddysgu a Llyfrgelloedd

This item should be returned or renewed by the
last date stamped below.

Newport
CITY COUNCIL
CYNGOR DINAS
Casnewydd

ls

D1514382

To renew visit:
www.newport.gov.uk/libraries

VV
FRANKLIN WATTS
LONDON•SYDNEY

Franklin Watts

First published in Great Britain in 2015 by The Watts Publishing Group

Copyright © 2015 The Watts Publishing Group

All rights reserved.

Series editor: Julia Bird
Series consultant: Catherine Glavina
Series designer: Peter Scoulding

Every attempt has been made to clear copyright. Should there be any inadvertent omission please apply to the publisher for rectification.

Picture acknowledgements: Arco Images GmbH/Alamy: 18-19, 22tl. © Arterra Picture Library/Alamy. Baron b/Shutterstock: 14-15, 22br. Mikkel Bigandt/Shutterstock: 20-21. Richard Clark/istockphoto: 4bc. Peter Elvridge/Shutterstock: 4tl. Eric Gevaert/Shutterstock: 4bl. Neil Roy Johnson/Shutterstock: 5br. KUNPISIT/Shutterstock: 22tr. Lodimup/Shutterstock: 8-9, 22bl. marlee/Shutterstock: 11. Pavelk/Shutterstock: 4tc. PCHT/Shutterstock: front cover. Perfect Lazybones/Shutterstock: 1, 12-13, 22cr. Catalin Petola /Shutterstock: 6. Ppaauullee/Shutterstock: 5tr.

HB ISBN: 978 1 4451 3862 6
PB ISBN: 978 1 4451 3864 0
Library ebook ISBN: 978 1 4451 3863 3

Dewey number: 599

Printed in China

Franklin Watts
An imprint of
Hachette Children's Group
Part of The Watts Publishing Group
Carmelite House
50 Victoria Embankment
London EC4Y 0DZ

An Hachette UK Company
www.hachette.co.uk

www.franklinwatts.co.uk

MIX
Paper from
responsible sources
FSC
www.fsc.org
FSC® C104740

Newport Community Learning & Libraries	
X010597	
PETERS	22-Dec-2016
J636	£6.99

Contents

On the
farm

There are lots of animals to meet on the farm.

Clucking chickens

Chickens are birds. Female chickens lay eggs. Some eggs hatch into chicks.

Swimming
ducks

Ducks are birds that swim. They have shiny feathers.

Chewing
COWS

Cows make milk to feed their babies. We drink their milk too.

11

Nosy
pigs

Pigs are very good at smelling things. They have long noses called snouts.

Woolly
sheep

Sheep have
thick coats made
of wool. We
use the wool to
make jumpers.

Busy goats

Goats love to jump and climb!

We drink goat's milk and eat cheese made from it.

1

Big horses

Horses are very strong. They can carry a person or pull a cart.

Farm
dogs

Some dogs help
on the farm. They
keep groups of
sheep together.

Word bank

 Cart

Eggs

 Shiny feathers

Snout

 Wool

Quiz

1. Female chickens lay

a) apples
b) eggs
c) bananas.

2. Pigs have long noses called

a) trunks
b) horns
c) snouts.

3. Goats love to

a) wiggle and jiggle
b) dance and sing
c) jump and climb.

Turn over for answers!

Notes for adults

TADPOLES are structured to provide support for newly independent readers. The books may also be used by adults for sharing with young children.

Starting to read alone can be daunting. **TADPOLES** help by providing visual support and repeating words and phrases. These books will both develop confidence and encourage reading and rereading for pleasure.

If you are reading this book with a child, here are a few suggestions:

1. Make reading fun! Choose a time to read when you and the child are relaxed and have time to share the book.

2. Talk about the content of the book before you start reading. Look at the front cover and blurb. What expectations are raised about the content? Why might the child enjoy it? What connections can the child make with their own experience of the world?

3. If a word is phonically decodable, encourage the child to use a 'phonics first' approach to tackling new words by sounding the words out.

4. Invite the child to talk about the content after reading, returning to favourite pages and pictures. Extend vocabulary by examining the Word Bank and by discussing new concepts.

5. Give praise! Remember that small mistakes need not always be corrected.

Answers

Here are the answers:

1.b 2.c 3.c

Index